INDIE ROCK

INDIE ROCK

JOE BISHOP

UNIVERSITY
of ALBERTA
PRESS

Published by
UNIVERSITY OF ALBERTA PRESS
1-16 Rutherford Library South
11204 89 Avenue NW
Edmonton, Alberta, Canada T6G 2J4
amiskwaciwâskahikan | Treaty 6 | Métis Territory
uap.ualberta.ca | uapress@ualberta.ca

Library and Archives Canada Cataloguing in Publication
Title: Indie rock / Joe Bishop.
Names: Bishop, Joe, 1975– author.
Series: Robert Kroetsch series.
Description: Series statement: Robert Kroetsch series
Identifiers: Canadiana (print) 20220454604 | Canadiana (ebook) 20220454612 |
     ISBN 9781772126785 (softcover) | ISBN 9781772126990 (EPUB) |
     ISBN 9781772127003 (PDF)
Subjects: LCGFT: Poetry.
Classification: LCC PS8603.I85 I53 2023 | DDC C811/.6—dc23

First edition, first printing, 2023.
First printed and bound in Canada by Houghton Boston Printers,
     Saskatoon, Saskatchewan.
Copyediting by Kimmy Beach.
Proofreading by Mary Lou Roy.

A volume in the Robert Kroetsch Series.

University of Alberta Press gratefully acknowledges the support received for its pub-
lishing program from the Government of Canada, the Canada Council for the Arts,
and the Government of Alberta through the Alberta Media Fund.

CONTENTS

I

PATRICK STREET ON ST. PADDY'S DAY

My heartfelt player, rock star in recovery,
chain-vaping comrade, mainstream loner,
'neath the mink sheen of young locks you let grow,
though I've grown sick of your wisecracks, Mike,
I'd still like to swill whiskey with you at your
magnetic muss of a bedsit on Patrick Street,
where I could feel close as you finger your
old acoustic with the string missing,
where I could demonstrate my amusement
at your falsetto, riff a flippant face,
where I could confess my legend till you bleed,
where you could pull off an accentuating dress
instead of those constricting red slacks, Mike.
Tell me how you kink, how you've harmed,
how many panties dropped, how much mush,
expound on the hell of your righteous shame,
where we could dirty sheets in your dryer, Mike,
where it's us, not the rest of the pagan galaxy
or those moist sardines packed at Green Sleeves,
where it's only us and the cairn of our sighs.

LIVE AT THE BATTERY

Strap on axe / sapphire-chromed
Step out through open window
Plug in atop the kitchen roof
Tune gloaming / windswept Narrows

Swig the Jack / stomp on fuzz
Swing at / chop saltwater air
Gulp feedback / gain aftertaste
Vamp / tap / drone / burp / timber

Chomp barre chord / raise the rock
Slay the giant with plastic pick
Bend / slide the spirit sword
Hallelujah / right hooks / lefts

Jack whammy / get biblical
Till bergs in Cuckold's Cove quake
Lick the neck with furcate tongue
Wah wah / ooh babe / slash / shred / rake

Tower topples / watch falling rock
From rubble glean hardcore riffs
A black gull building above reverb
Hammers on / squawks on / no bridge

Red beams flashing from the hillside
To guide ships in the harbour
Amplify while dusk's pyro ends
Crank / honk / blast / faster / louder

CARPENTRY

Logging
is still high risk.
Mike, let me strip
your bark,
dress you in silty
Speedos,
vintage gold
medals,
nail you
behind a forest fire.
Let me brush you taller than
birch, Mike,
wearing only my
flashy sperm
and leather
tool belt
(the lighthouse strobing
cliff
backdrop, charcoal
afterglow)
draw you
up close
to killer whales,
plastered bergs
collapsing
now, or
eclipsed, a sketchy
stickman.
Let me bevel you into
a shell, Mike,
shave you
into my scrimshaw.

DEVIL-MA-CLICK

I's the b'y who cloistered
with cans of Canadian
till I rose from the wing chair,
left corbels and wainscoting.

I's the b'y who sheared wool,
strung yarn and knitted mitts,
to keep me hands from freezing
when I axed the fiddle's spruce.

I's the b'y who fiddled her,
dismembered her for splits,
burnt her with furled burls,
winded squeeze-box bellows.

I's the b'y who came flanked
by jigs and reels, by corroded
organ flues and a dead fish
plant, here to raise the Avalon.

AFTER A THREE-MONTH FRIENDSHIP

A humble breeze replaced the evening mist
We sat on your conforming concrete step
Night crept by and you worked a morning shift

We'd just finished your chicken curry dish
I lit my cigarette and passed the Bic
A humble breeze replaced the evening mist

You reminded me of my independence
I could fuck off on planes and hit cities
Night crept by and you worked a morning shift

Flicking butts we stood to hug pre-exit
Your stubble shot feels down my stifled prick
A humble breeze replaced the evening mist

As we squeezed it planted against my neck
Beneath the moon the blindside of your peck
Night crept by and you worked a morning shift

My frisson grew from your impulsive gift
It took testicles and holy spirit
A humble breeze replaced the evening mist
Night crept by and you worked a morning shift

AFTER OUR AA MEETING

I pulled over to drop Joy off
But she asked me in, for tea.
I asked if she had stronger.
Single malt, she said.

Joy lit candles in the living room,
Turned on a turntable. Needle
Spun his adenoidal tenor—
True love leaves no traces.

Joy held my arm on a loveseat.
Tumbler's volume rose.
Why're you applying makeup?
It's just lipstick. She winked.

I nuzzled her elfin auricle,
Inhaled her eucalyptus lozenge.
It dissolved in precursory kisses,
In our struggling mouths.

Our tongues staggered. I unclasped
A-cups. Joy flipped
The vinyl, hooked me
To rug, took me by her coffee table,

Arched, oohed, gnawed my lip,
Surrendered to her wall of sound,
As the ladies' man cried
Don't go home with your hard-on.

QUITTING

After three years, Mike,
Why did I compare
My nicotine patch

To chemical castration,
After three years, Mike,
After you dangled

Back-to-back texts—
Got any plans today?
Really horny here.

I've craved a chance
To drop any plans;
Even now I wait to run

My hands through your hair,
After three years, Mike,
After three long years.

CONCEPTION BAY WOMAN

I held the ear of smoking cup,
touched stiff pucker to brim,

sipped her naked tea.
Redbreast whistles tickled a spider.

Linen load pinned to line caught
spindrift's warp and woof.

I rode bitch on the quad she
backed up at a threadbare bridge.

Hot engine, intricate cliff
drove my loins to salivate.

Mad rock knifed gravid wave.
I picked her a pitcher plant,

drowned in her leaf, died
for her carnivorous swallow.

DON'T WORRY ABOUT ME, MIKE

I charged over cobbles in jubilee,
swaggered at the pub, cast in wrought iron,
mined supernovas as skirts fanned emerald facets,
but don't worry about me, Mike,

don't worry about me.
Not long after midnight my fist broke.
Queasy dawn deposited leaden knocks.
Horny vein above my brow would throb till I threw up.

O how I miss them homicidal times.
Luckily, I've got funds in no accounts.
Besides, I'm as good as dead or better off.
But don't worry about me, Mike,

don't worry about me.
My dry dreams of drinking with you
in this petrified cot, in these death throes,
under a blanket of monastic clamour, consume,

but, Mike, don't worry about me,
my famines prosper like cloistered ore.
While druids consolidate Wicker Man glamour
with serpentine gold, I offer my propitiatory peat,

conjure clastic jingles, do without the dance
that twirls my guts, without a shamrock paperweight,
but don't worry about me, don't go
fretting over me, Mike, please.

I kill wormy mornings training in martial arts,
hollow out rainy afternoons for cutthroat marathons.
My meteoric larynx gives long before oak legs let go.
O Mike, don't worry about me.

I blast breakneck platitudes past abstinent tadpoles,
mourn my Milky Way of little deaths.
The heat of licks from effigies bedevils
but, Michael Peter Seamus, don't worry about me.

PARADE STREET DUO (APRIL FOOLS)

Balled up, she hogs our clammy quilt. Awake—
goose-fleshed, ossified, throbbing—I detach
from mattress, raise roman shade: snare-drum rain
on glass, Basilica's noon bongs calling.
A drop ticks—numinous—in a bucket.
Staves of verse and chorus sheet chilled floorboards.
I'm twitching, wearing briefs, rolling the last
of my stash on her hard-cover of nudes.
I stone bronchi, amuse demons—but look,
she trembles. Christ, it leads me to believe
comedown off green rappels next to the nose-
dive from her night of bumps, her highbrow lines.
She grunts strung-out blues. Our box spring bugles.
Response?—my muted prayer: give us your cue.

TIME-LAPSE (FIRST SLEEPOVER)

I bust green on your atlas with Swiss Army
Knife scissors, roll, spark, take hits to lung caves.

I exhale moths, burn bat down to the cork,
in bed with you, primed to watch *Manhattan*.

I pounce, tickle ribs. Your freckled breasts
wobble while you writhe, feign hating it.

I inhale your clean, dryer-exhaust sweat,
slide over to the smoggy side. You sigh,

rest your sunset on my monochrome chest.
Rhapsody in Blue's glissando takes flight.

Mariel Hemingway tells Woody not
everyone gets corrupted. While you feel

under the covers for remote, "Embrace-
able You" panders. Credits. Click. It's dark.

MEDLEY FOR MY BANSHEE

*

Your keen wakes goldfish.
Your voice picks my ossicles,
Octaves purple with lupins.

*

You pitch banker's lamp
At my dodging noggin.
I fear for the alarm clock.

*

Watching *Wheel of Fortune*,
I howl mad guesses
Just to make you laugh.

*

You wear your mermaid gown,
Clutch a bunch of black roses,
Your freckles powdered,

In a photo on the mantel,
Protected behind glass.

BARELY AUDIBLE LAMENT

Entering the bathroom, I noticed
the clacking racket the venetian blind
made in the window our thesaurus
held ajar, before I saw the tub, or her, or red.

I lugged her out, caught a whiff of rust from spilling
iron. I heard a faraway foghorn blow
and a foghorn faintly blew from my recording.
My wordless dirge required strained ears.

Her eyes fixated on the ceiling fan. The algae
between her lashes I still see in monochrome.
Looking back, I may have imagined
the roric *I'm sorry* fingered on the mirror.

With terrible treble I tried to capture
how my cortex distorted her coiffure
of tangled kelp. My adrenaline moshed against
lactic acid. Tiny hairs spiked like my Mohawk.

I'm sure I winced while wrapping her wrist
and I tried to make the listener wince a little.
I smudged the phone, forced our address
past snapping molars. Later, I shredded.

My tempo made up for lacking loudness.
Siren decibels maxed. Ruby flashes strobed.
Paramedics performed. I went to work on tritones.
I etched Satanic rock, nightlong, in the dark.

In a wingback, in the living room, with booze
on my breath, I fretted my unplugged Strat at a loss
for lyrics, and I picked until I passed out.
This instrumental I gave her Christian name.

LOWDOWN, LOWDOWN

Waiting on her bench by the bay window,
Waiting like a sailor's wife, seconds chipping,
She'd scribble black phrases on bars,
Claw copper wire out of her scalp,
Claw jarring jangles from careworn piano keys,
Waiting to snort a brief supply.

From her great grandmother's
We shipped that played-out heirloom here.
Here it stands out in our front room
Like an old saloon prop, like it might
Plunk "The Entertainer" by itself; instead
It stands upright with the lid shut.

I wait on her bench for my lift to arrive,
I wait for the drive to the recovery centre.
I'll hand over stained Hanes to a social worker,
Squat after she searches my bag;
The nurses will patronize in ivory pitches.
I'll hear the grave left hand weigh

Down *The Young and The Restless* theme,
Read verse wrought with motley platitudes
And bad grammar on bulletin boards,
Bunk with a junkie's bottomless armpit reek.
He'll share abominations and with a flimsy pillow
Hush me, paranoid I might sing.

WE IDLED AT THE SHIP

We idled at the Ship, owned Captain's rum.
Hyperbole assailed as we blasphemed
our head doctors. Soaring on park swings,
we kicked legs out and took October's moon.

We cuddled our insomnia in tunes.
The night that owned you had my thumb flushing
your vodka, Ativan. In the Psych wing,
I sifted past a howling Haldol scrum,

past cemetery stares; you were in the bowels,
wearing a saffron robe bruised with inkblots.
You opened up, let air your dreams of blood,

words of the dead behind cinder-block walls.
There, you embarked, tackled petrified rot,
the sewage, on a voyage, up-close, abroad.

BOXING DAY (CABIN FEVER)

I give a junk to stove, tune Celtic mandolin,
skate down its neck. The kerosene-lit wick
mirrors picks on lenses of her Buddy Holly specs.
Sleet pings clapboard. Wine blurs her saucy lips
and salty cheekbones. She checks her phone
for a miracle of signals. With knuckles tucked
under fleecy sleeves, she wipes fog off pane,
peers at the unseen pond's gusty nocturne,
cites August: knee deep, I'd dived—disrupting
my solo to sketch out how I wobbled back on feet,
red trickling from the hairline down my nose.
Remember you said you felt woozy? Cackles
eclipse her lunar laughs. I entertain smashing
glasses, plucking eyes needed for passion plays.

ASH WEDNESDAY

I took a hit, first toke in seven years.
Collapsed ashes kissed bathwater,
near the last of the alabaster bubbles.

I imagined my gnarly dotage, shrivelled,
restrained in a restraining chair.
Would distortions from dementia force

flashbacks of her unforced giggles,
prompting my dusty lips to stretch a smile?
How long had I forgotten how to laugh at

our first gig, playing live at the Ship—
false start after false start and re-tuning,
the dry strums of dry runs, her voice

travelling like a flung accordion
evaporates over rocks down a rocky hill?
How long did I smoke in that tub before

I unplugged dregs to the demon who inspired
behind walls, who hummed through pipes,
the devil whose love she rejoiced in?

REMEMBRANCE DAY

Shell shock, they called it, when the Regiment,
who, returned to harbour life, couldn't keep
a barbed wire synapse from a barbed wire trench,
flash from optic nerve, who couldn't keep

ear canals from fugal melee, scud
of artillery at bay, fellers slugged,
knelt stiff beside them in the pelted mud
that churned arms and regurgitated blood.

All the shaming in the world couldn't shrink
malignant cracks; no volt out-shocked trauma.
In airtight rooms the wish for death increased
like battlefields had bred bacteria.

Dr. Freud got drafted to reconsider.
Eli Lilly vied to rout disorder.

CANADA DAY PYRO

Bounding from boulder
to boulder, we both land on one

the same time, bang
salmon shoulders. Rubbing

hurt, we redden. Driftwood
sparks. Sunshine splits

inukshuk. Frisky capelin
kill themselves. Then

sudden waves shiver deeper navy,
whip Noxzema nose-caps;

flinty fog unloads, buries
kelp, and gusts forge

a gale, but no gale can cancel
lupins from swelling, two rockets.

YANKEE BOYS OF ARGENTIA

I grew up beside an American Naval Base.
They called us Newfs; we called them Yanks, though

Many stationed came with Southern drawls.
I'd befriend Virginian brats like Peter York.

I'd crave the nicotine that tanned his teeth,
Laissez-faire vowels, taking their time on his tongue,

More than the stockpile of switchblades he smuggled.
I aped how Peter sloped like he favoured wounds,

Envied each Camel his thumb and index pinched.
I wish I could repeat his twisted jody calls.

He traded *Penthouse* pets and *Playboy* bunnies.
Stains of his tributes stuck on centrefolds.

Peter served as fodder for filthy dreams of freedom.
We would kill our Sundays tenpin bowling.

DANCE SONG

Before George Michael made visits to johns
For jollies chic in a cheeky dance song,

On our island, dozen after dozen,
Entrapped men behind stall doors had fun in

The Village Shopping Mall. I watched every
Evening, the square-jawed anchorman reveal

Names, air photos, clips of the men in cuffs,
Blab till the weather with neutered disgust.

A note passed in class outed my neighbour
In the next row, marked him as a nephew.

It snowballed to a shit-knocking at lunch.
He wore a scarlet scrap of his uncle's brunt.

FARM MUSEUM FUNDRAISER

Speaker thanked you, James, at St. Teresa's,
where you sold raffle tickets—Protestant
treasurer patting Catholics—before
joining Anne, who waited at a communal
table for a waiter to serve the rye
bread that came with lamb stew. Raised near pastures
of fated grazers, Anne abstained from them
chopped. You goaded her, James, but Anne refused
to sip your Guinness broth; instead she bit
the yellowed slice, tempered blushing hunger,
reminded herself you tally funds for a cause
close to her rustic roots. Wary of growls
behind attire, of slaughter, Anne held back
an Abrahamic judgement of your nudge.

HEAVE-UP SONG

Once Johnny got a taste for cod tongues he couldn't keep within
quotas. He couldn't stop stogging his face, topping off with lobster
claws and rabbit hearts, topping off with scrunchions, toutons,
turrs, ptarmigan, bottled moose, flipper pies, potatoes as good as
apples, cabbage mulched with capelin, and buckets and buckets
of salt meat. Johnny puffed up like a sculpin, bulged out like The
Newfoundland Blob, before he heaved the lot of scoffs, before he
heaved gravy and gurry, gull guts and buttercups, granite brine
in his veins, mussels in his corner, essential offshore oil, crude
and primal Screech, pony piss, vinegar, tartar, jamjams, molasses,
blueberry grunt, diabetic shock, before he heaved his bottleneck
genes. He whittled to an isthmus. Johnny drooled for game pronged
on tines, longed to lick the head of a just-pulled pint which tastes
as good as Satan's seed but his island made him seasick, served up
nothing but dry heaves.

DIRTY NEWFOUNDLANDERS

Rose is known up the shore
Mostly for her buoy-knockers
Bold Elizabeth is known for
Hitting on abortion doctors

Face and eyes in Sally's fork
Now the heel and now the toe
Lovely tell your mother Jack
Pack your grips and let her go

Harry rubs his horses raw
Tommy deepthroats rotten cod
Bill Dicks dildos all the b'ys
With curious lobster claws

Face and eyes in Sally's fork
Now the heel and now the toe
Sure 'tis wonderful grand by Jove
Pack your grips and let her go

Boiled-boot Marg at the factory
Is hardtack and dry as the bicky
But her tits leak Purity syrup
And she'll lay mint knobs d'rackly

Face and eyes in Sally's fork
Now the heel and now the toe
Inside-out in jig time Joe
Pack your grips and let her go

EVENING ON LIVINGSTONE STREET

On a lit burner, Colin heats the hot
knives. Nate takes a hit and passes creaming
blonde to me. I decline, plug in earbuds.
Patti Smith talks of horses, audible
to Colin and to Nate, who adjusts his wig
in a compact mirror, takes another hit,
applies shadow to lids, induces sfumato,
brushes Natalie to life, then switches
off a bald bulb hanging by cord overhead.
She leaves a print of her fuckered lips on my
shaved pate, toddles off to a cab in pumps.
I punch lips in drywall, smear my knuckles
ruby. Colin retires to another room,
plasters tissue with upshots of arousal.

GARY

Gary brought it to my attention, lying
nude on my made bed. His index finger

spiralled my nude bicep. Gazing, he inquired
into the tinkling sound. I confessed

I didn't know where it came from. He left
traces on my tongue and duvet. I didn't hear

tinkling for nights but tonight
there is just enough breeze, not unlike

the tinkling breeze that night I blew
and rimmed Gary and it bothered me and

it bothered me more and then
I got out of bed, tracked chimes down.

I cut them from my neighbour's line.
They lie like marionettes on my nightstand.

FATHER'S DAY

I haul on his rubber boots,
pack tackle box aboard, part
glinting pond on which my old
man taught me how to skate.

My grown hands recoil,
recalling numb, small fingers
tighten laces to his standard.
This morning suns knuckles.

I bait hook, cast lured line,
scratch what will be beard,
relive one morning when
I was five and Dad took me

here ice-fishing. He didn't trust
further out, laid down stick,
ordered: do not pass. Boring
auger, his glance caught me

gliding past, caught rot-hole
snatching. Submerged in the
jolt of his hand hooking hood,
our teeth clacking, I reel.

He woke me nights later,
casting wails down the hall,
hauled from dream's outcome,
moral for sons who won't listen.

GOOSEBERRY COVE

Below a starry
sunroof
we strip
in his pickup as its
beams beam milk
from shore.
Our soles
slip on spit pebbles.
Spindrift pecks
sisterly.
Atlantic leather
belts us.
Nips nip feet
under frigid quilts.
We clam up.
We clench fists.
Starfish
embrace driftwood.

JINKER

Wore sleeves of ink crosses
Hoarded a hundred cats
Stowed son's scoring puck
Aboard his longliner
Never whistled in his life
Never even maimed a bird
Never named the Scottish play
And Friday was his Sunday
Now he lies with Davy Jones
Another ghost of Jonah

ROOT CELLAR BLUES

I built a root cellar O baby by our stone house on the bluff
Said I built a root cellar O darling by our stone house on the bluff
I stogged her tight with beets O sure beets you know you love

I carved and I cured planks O baby curved them into a hull
Said I carved and I cured planks O darling to curve them into a hull
I welded a dragger and spun nets O our Lab he did help haul

I fracked behind backs O had to find fuel for our stone home
Said I did frack behind backs O found the fuel for our stone home
Rigged a rig up O baby and drilled the heat for our stone home

But uproot you did O baby with that mainlander you took off
Said uproot you did O darling to that mainlander you just jetted off
O some feller from the Rockies while I watched contrails from the bluff

37

YOUNG FELLER'S TALE

Ne'er a flobber on the barrisway.
I heave a dead man's dive,
Fadder's sod, born on Outer Ring.
He cut cord, drove past overpass.

I roved with he and Mudder past
lichen-claimed graves, beaver dams
rigged from crabapple trees.
We climbed tolts, traipsed gullies,

waded through bog, weaved
erratics, the stunted tuckamores
over barrens, and tangled in pines.
Maggoty nippers nipped.

Roots flipped me arse over kettle.
Mudder smooched where it smert.
We made ne'er a queak
stitching warmth from pelts.

I sparked splits come duckish.
Brindy boughs crackled and creamed.
Flankers sprayed from junks I dropped.
Fadder spun one of his yarns.

He'd tell of his spell in a whale,
how his bites dug floors of blubber,
how he built a flue up blow hole.
Pay he no heed, Mudder'd say.

I jillick mid a screecher of gulls.
Humpbacks blast and gush
to fathom the sun's harpoons.
The sea sings her hooks in me deeps.

LITTLE SEA-SONG

Father, I glom on to seafarer fear
like some horseshoe forged before the wars, or
a souvenir, them rusty hooks we found,
dear dad, who dwells on turf and still afar,
while dandelions rise to reflect dawn,
adrift in a boat with your cloudy breath,
catching dumb cod, and you revive, old man
done with old wives' tales, and though the voyage
never carried out as hoped, and I drowned
once I sank with the longliner, as hard
as I hold on to my name, we both know
no longer that stout sailor then was I
those years ago, and one year drags to ten
when decay turns to decades in clean bone.

OVERTURE

When hailstones bang stained glass
When castrati trill on spasmodic panes
When eunuchs crack and branch out
When antlers flash and cathedrals collapse
When timpani rumble undergrowth
When bleating tritones corral oaks from earth
When airy mares ram soppy rafters
When hooves kick can-can crescendos
When spans of cloud come galloping past
When the storm blasts in surround sound
I strap on my Strat and hammer-on phrases
And maniac neighbours mend their flat fences
And chainsaws slash billets from fallen timber
And roofs reunite as strings bend to bridges

SALTBOX

Grandfather unreels his eyes out a new window.
His stare could hit bottom.
His stare wards off fog.
I ask him why the window used to be no

wider than a porthole.
He gives me a glare to answer that.
I've inherited his glower
but now he's handed down this old saltbox

with its new window gaping the harbour.
Grandfather's going in a home.
His rusted trunk is packed.
He doubts he'll be back here.

The stroke that struck turned him
askew as the davenport drooling
stuffing where his starched arm rests.
The other arm in increments climbs—

arthritic tow of brewing rain.
He soothes birch-broom whiskers,
recalls forking hay in a clammy barn
that tide has since undercut,

pictures Nan tending her rhubarb patch,
windswept on embankment since given to ebb.
Love's rudder steered her to dotage
before a blockage sunk her heart.

Her sewing kit and recipes rest here;
her salvaged nose for my saltwater air,
her green thumb stitched into mine,
given with the anchor of grandfather's stare.

DEAR DIGGER

Earth's eager for your fat beagle body,
to feed on your strained tendons, be
with bones older than the ones you've buried,
to read the works from your digest.
Curved not for incumbent beasts, earth
obeys the dirty laws of botany.

Through the numb soles of your splayed paws
do you divine earth's gravel voice?
Digger, spiking glucose makes you blind...
Or does her tenor woof poetic?
Cataracts fog your autumn lenses...

To also go where the best of you goes,
the haloed expanse where your vision stays,
Digger, my friend, this man can dream.

ARTY RELATIVE

My cousin starched inside his cadet uniform,
face fresh as the bay wind off Whiteway,
his hometown with its—*don't blink*—one road—
I picture that regimented boy while my mother
relays his adult battle against desire, desire
our common forefather, the hungry settler

who departed from the mother kingdom,
who sailed Anglo-Saxon codes to newfound land
and claimed his sod, the ghosts of our family tree,
untraceable nomads who had relied on legs
and the grace of God, brought with him, a fog
I go driving in just to go driving in, to pray

at the wheel for my cousin, blistered
in a room in Vancouver. I try not to dwell
on the incurable virus lurking in his veins,
weigh his poz status against his lust for free rein.
He will shake his bout of shingles, I chant,
make it a mantra, my tension lifting

at an intersection. But the stress he puts on
your auntie, my mother often comments,
while I follow his travels—meets in johns on jets,
visits to glory holes, his manic streaking
through a train station—captured by
bold globs portraying an ingrained redemption.

ENLIGHTENED POETS

We whistle up our own
attics, bawl away
in high chairs—

worse, an infant faith
in the garden
never to spring again.

Worse, silenced kittens
will only grow
the river colder.

Worse, lab technicians
never nicely
grab albino mice.

Worse, archive curators
cancel dates and
assign no time for folk.

Worse, wise humanists
laud lasers for
Aquarian guillotines.

DISSOCIATIVE SONG

swim amid dolphins
bleat by lambs

settle down to dirt
in a graveyard mulch

but you're doomed
hanging out at home

praise pyrotechnics
of synced bottlenoses

hail flocks that fled
shrines for paying debts

why fist your fins at
acrobatic semiotics

you've raised a church
of blackbird fugues

you've let a great gust
heave you far from home

OUTSIDER ART

As Orphée, my golden oldies crowded bowls.
When my neck splinters in the liberated river
as strings strike chords on unconscious rocks,
as I hunch in gnarled leather, drool, toothless,
with a tongue for tautology, a soul for gospel,
with fingers fractured, my muscles atrophied,
in spite, in short, in brief, in stocking feet, im-
merse in this dry aquarium, headbang along,
as my thrashing a cappella disturbs airwaves,
as clamps dangle from electrocuted nipples,
as lighting and makeup ennoble my sockets,
my life behind glass, in a castle with no toilet.

CELLULOID TANGO

God produced our grainy pigment.
I pencilled in horrorshow, chiaroscuro

of craggy cheek, framed in the strata
of a second. You mouthed

how an auteur reveals the fourth wall
by hiding Fabergé eggs, developed a taste for

matryoshki, mined guerrilla docs, gorged on
sulphur before that boom mic napalmed.

Our cutting room floor mapped chromatophores
from Limbo. Your Sisyphean climb

mimed deviations from the Method.
My Marlon Brando hammed, a glib klieg.

DANNY BOY

Dan, you asked me over to watch the world
premiere of *Thriller*. As MJ altered
from jerry-curled boyfriend to werewolf,
cries escaped you, my kindergarten friend.

Over your dad's duct-taped recliner hung
a famous portrait, the platinum-blonde Lord
painted in megawatts, as if he'd come
to light your living room, your trailer court.

Elvis, above us, rendered on velvet
with pompadour and silent baritone—
Danny, do you judge him as a pervert?
Believe an incognito king now roams?

I BELIEVE HE WOULD BELIEVE ME NOT COMPLETELY

If I told him I descended basement stairs
to fling the Bounce I forgot to fling in the dryer
if I let him sniff its infused bouquet
if I noted how footfall after footfall

on lacquered oak through threadbare socks
pressed cold against my pressing soles
how steps became a landing at the turn
if I mentioned the creaking bullnose

and the clusters of rust on the iron rail
and if I let a gyprock scene arrange itself
I believe he would believe me heretofore
but would he believe me would he

if I told him hares not there when I emptied the washer
now squished against beams and the hot water boiler
but not one hare a rabbit from Warner Bros
but not one sweet bunny laying eggs either

but hares with woodland tones and sandstone shades
but some ashen but some enriched in silver with
ears erected each horny but labial both
ears each pairs of moccasins each hollow

ear both seashell and gravy boat both
ears screwed to each head to heart to hare
but how would he believe me how would he
if I swore I gingerly I squeezed I between hares

and my legs below my knees completely disappeared
and I shuffled through furry furnaces through
traffic jams of revved engines focused
in idling sparks from the blacks of sound

eyes beaming breakneck hearts but mad
eyes breeding through March but blocked
eyes blocked from eyeing the wondrous moon
and I wonder would he wonder if I announced

I never knew such desolate desolation until then
and also such abundant abundant abundance
radiating from those radiating hares
crammed-in and carnal there for no reasonable reason

and no room to budge and stuck springing
in place or trading captive places and hares
and hares everywhere with their restless
noses but why did I pick one up and release it

through the open window open below the ceiling
while my cotton-blend unmentionables
tumbled like teeming salmon down the dryer drum
and the hare replicated when I turned around

there the hare I freed to freedom
and I mean there the same godforsaken hare
but when I bent to snatch it up again
the hare punched with ears pinned back

and scratched and scratched both my bare arms
and if I do not tell him what will I tell him
in case I show him the scratch marks
I would have to in good faith to straight-up tell him

but would he believe me if I declared
the Byronic one with two cloven hooves
and his loyal rebels cast down from clouds
hustled on the concrete floor instead of hares

and offered slices filled with a taste for gnosis
and Baudelaire warned like a prophet
and would he believe me if I confessed
to bricks of hashish stashed under my bed

along with an unsold copy of *Les Paradis artificiels*
but would he tune in if I streamed
the basement striking its set and staging
the first automatic garden after the word *let*

or deepening deeper than the deepest depth
or doing nothing at all after all it did
but he would believe my visions and my revisions
and my conditions in this condition

if only he assumed what I assumed
and who knows I guessed maybe who knows
no constricted hares did materialize there
but would he believe a word in sent texts

if I deleted the idioms of my body would he
if I muted the tones in my throat would he
and there for a second and a second there I saw
Factory portraits grace the musty basement

but how would silkscreens explain my marks
and how would these hands hold a hot hare not there
but I began to doubt again and saw
Monroes replaced by Mansons replaced by

an orchestra orchestrating the Largo by Dvořák
going on and on and going on and on
and what if I phoned him and emphatically bawled
or voiced that pig that stutters that that is all folks

instead of stating nothing happened
to matter more than my laundry gone
from the banging spin to the cool down
and the vanishing act of vulgar stains

and finally the spiritual finally petered out as
if an untraceable hand had vaporwave fade out as
if Deadmau5 had the house adjust to dying air
but what if I hammered out hymns for him

and what if I named the unnamable One
who knew each hair on his hitherto hairy head
who knew every livelong whisker
on every hare erased from the basement

V

VICTORIA DAY IN HEART'S DELIGHT

I drove from town last night,
arriving later than expected.
Cops had roadblocks up.
I flicked panel's main switch,

but was soon tingled to sleep
by rain's sizzle on steep shingles.
It stopped when I woke.
I lit the wood stove. Her damper

gaped. Birch warmed as rays
adumbrated the harbour, inked
sky imperial blue. Chomping
burnt toast that dripped Ever-

sweet oleo, rocking a rocker
by the window, I saw John
step from his truck onto
wharf, velcro glowing suit

over flannel, swap Nikes for
rubbers; his crepuscular shift
toward a lobster fisherman.
I watched John load the traps.

TOUCHING LINES

My name, I find, engraved beside my brother's,
marking an August day, last century,
hands-on hours when we found spikes for carving
in this cove of bedrock not much wider than

St. Matthew's altar. Shoulder blades press against
incline of strewn slab. I wedge (a cyborg
of sorts) near spiders who dip in pooling craters.
Words on my app autocorrect as I spell-out—

playing house with cousins—our unrestraint
assembled these slabs to tables, turned the shale
to plates, crag to cabinet—or when house

was church—my brother, best man or Reverend—
once I stood in as bride—now I enter the word
fossil—fingerprints impinge on glass.

INHERITED THUMBNAIL

Hominid-handled bovine bone hammered
Kindred skull. No dragging knuckles stopped
Him looting dark markets, the self helped
To fat figs, muted chops of choice tapir.

Early man made primal maul, hammered
Raft and drifted. Shrooming troglodyte asked
Great Mother why clubs had to clobber trans-
Animal cavemen, interspecies lovers.

Deckhand heard whale codas click; they hammered
Hull all night. Till gory dusk he'd hauled
Dragging line, deftly stroked but dreamed

An earthy bed. Jack fathomed his lure to the spear,
Sensed he'd still sniff sperm after moulting
His oilskin, slow withdrawal of his dogged sea-legs.

NUCLEAR RUNOFF

Headlong beard, break-
                       neck shush of whitewater, broadens
downriver and this flickery red-
                              breast warbles from a birch limb
sleeved in silver
                  thaw, heckles the New York comic who, straight-
faced, strips, streaks slap-
                       dash up the blue snow-
bank and for a thread-
                     bare bit, trips, bombs
through pearly jolts of debacle, tatters
                                the rapids, then eddies
punch tendons
                 tart, black humour blind-
siding his nostrils, breath held
                         under arrest. The dead-
pan stand-up flails against drag, comes
                           back, tattooed
in katakana, in blotchy scripts, lets
                       wound-up teeth
chatter, cracks no grin, rusts
                     but that robin whistles a torch
song for its encore, previews his radio-
                       active spasms shatter
crystallized flop
                sweat, those shocked soles over-
lap starchy prints, him
                  reprise his Little Boy routine.

LAPS AT THE UNIVERSITY POOL

Years since my last swim. I lean on the ledge,
catch breath, haul goggles off, eye incoming

jock geared to jet, his breakneck limbs, propelled
shoulder blades, his piston-sinew. His soles

kick wall: strokes streamline; immaculately
timed flips, deep thrusts. The bucking butterfly

pilots, violates the parallel lane.
My rump floats. Chlorine's caustic aroma

drags me back to when I swam on the team,
shaving the peach fuzz off stopwatch faces.

Meets collide: whistle-blast echoed and we
warped ceiling lights below, spading water.

I outpaced peripherals to finish
where my linear ship soared, with hurrah.

OFF SEASON PITCH

This untreated sport I play endures despite the World
Series game over. Vacant dugout
teems with homeless leaves. Clutch hitters
spit hulls in their safe manspaces. Try on this mask,

catch my chill. A tipsy instrumentalist airs his long-held
piss which was stored in an organ so foul
you'll want to squint. An omniscient
announcer calls the braille of sleet. It's not even evening

but floodlights are vital. Bob these bad apples,
buy my proverbial crackerjacks
while your crenellated pumpkin-grin slides.

Who else will save faith for Black Friday?
Who else will wear their mitt to my warm-up prayer?
What fun advent awaits us come December?

RELEASE

After Elizabeth Bishop's "The Fish"

Drafted for battles he fought,
the fish won against men and,
now, hanging by lip corner
from her hook, half in water,
nearing half of her century,
he awaited award of rubber's
bash against bloodied gills.
Awed by what light caught,
she, an orphan of the world,
stared noninvasively inside
averted saucers and decided.
She held her overdue veteran,
declared a vision of victory,
let her speckled trophy live.

PINNACLE OR

Arctic-hued atef
or Vishnu-blue
or runic bone horn
atop Thor calving

out of Greenland
adrift in the harbour
or capstone breaching
by the thundering Jesus

or Enki shedding scales
or papal fish-hat erosion
or Tiamat primed to founder

to shine with a wound in June
to hiss and growl abroad in bits
to drown like a whimper in brine

SCRUPULOUS MUSIC

we cannot help
but see
all problems

through a filter
of faith
in the word,

a small, sharp stone
stabbing,
eyes thorny,

but we savour
the root,
scrupulum,

diagnosis
exact,
the solace,

hearing our name
cried out
from dark skies.

EAST COAST TRAIL, MIDNIGHT

I suck baffling wind, tap on
light app, hike
man-made steps cut in

bedrock, then the high
tangle, exult over mud's
tug, twig-crackling

footfalls, atop
the cliff, haul off
boots, drop

glowing phone to surf's
ecstatic swoosh, climb
God-given erratic, let

my moony sigh whet, let
that osprey adjust
its optics on me, whistle.

NOTES

"Live at The Battery"

The Battery: made up of colourful homes nested into the side of Signal Hill, it's the first neighbourhood you'll see when entering St. John's harbour.

"Devil-Ma-Click"

Devil-ma-click: adroit, versatile worker; jack of all trades (*Dictionary of Newfoundland English*).

Avalon: Avalon Peninsula, Newfoundland and Labrador.

"Dirty Newfoundlanders"

Inspired by a traditional folk song, "The Dirty Newfoundlanders."

"Jinker"

Jinker: an unlucky person.

"Young Feller's Tale"

Definitions for Newfoundland words can be found in the *Dictionary of Newfoundland English*, or at www.heritage.nf.ca/dictionary.

Outer Ring: highway on the outskirts of St. John's.

Overpass: first overpass leaving St. John's on the TransCanada Highway. To drive past the overpass is to leave the city, enter rural territory.

"Victoria Day in Heart's Delight"

Town: used frequently to refer to the capital city, St. John's.

"Pinnacle Or"

Pinnacle: type of iceberg that has a spire.

ACKNOWLEDGEMENTS

"Patrick Street on St. Paddy's Day" appeared in *Gasher Journal*, Summer 2022.

"Dance Song" appeared under the title "Nothing New Under the Sun" in *Bealtaine Magazine*, Issue 2, Spring 2022.

"Lowdown, Lowdown" appeared in *The Dillydoun Review*, Issue 11, December 2021.

"Inherited Thumbnail" appeared in *Plenitude Magazine*, November 2021.

"Medley for My Banshee" appeared in *Jersey Devil Press*, Issue 114, October 2021.

"Carpentry" and "Yankee Boys of Argentia" appeared in *The Puritan*, Issue 54, Summer 2021.

"East Coast Trail, Midnight" appeared in *Black Flowers*, Volume 10, Summer 2021.

"Father's Day," "dissociative song,""Victoria Day in Heart's Delight," "Touching Lines," "Inherited Thumbnail," "Nuclear Runoff" (under the title "Runoff"), "Off Season Pitch," "Release," and "Pinnacle Or" appeared in the chapbook *Dissociative Songs* (Frog Hollow Press, 2021).

"Young Feller's Tale" and "Touching Lines" appeared in *Innisfree Poetry Journal*, Issue 30, Spring 2020.

"Time-Lapse (First Sleepover)" appeared in *Tar River Poetry*, Volume 59, Number 2, Spring 2020.

"Outsider Art" appeared in *The Metaworker*, Fall 2019.

"Ash Wednesday" appeared *in Pattern Recognition*, Number 4, Summer 2019.

"Live at The Battery" appeared in *Poetry Is Dead*, Issue 18, Fall/Winter 2018.

"Conception Bay Woman," "Saltbox" (under the title "Saltbox, Heart's Delight-Islington"), and "Victoria Day in Heart's Delight," appeared in *Riddle Fence*, Issue 29, Spring 2018.

"Father's Day" appeared in *Plenitude Magazine*, January 2018, and is featured on the League of Canadian Poets' website (2020).

"We Idled at the Ship" and "Farm Museum Fundraiser" appeared in
Acta Victoriana, Volume 143, Number 1, Fall 2018.
"Overture," "Release," and "Pinnacle Or" appeared in *Former
People*, Summer 2018, as did "Celluloid Tango" under the title
"Celluloid Fauvism."
"Heave-Up Song" appeared in *In/Words Magazine & Press*, Volume
17, Issue 2, Spring 2018.
"Remembrance Day," under the title "Shell Shock," received a
Newfoundland and Labrador Arts and Letters poetry award
in 2016.
"Gooseberry Cove" appeared in *The New Quarterly*, Issue 95, Fall
2005.

Many thanks to everyone at University of Alberta Press, especially
my editor, Kimmy Beach, and the two anonymous jurors who
selected *Indie Rock* for publication. Thank you also to John Barton
and to my boyfriend, James Price.

OTHER TITLES FROM UNIVERSITY OF ALBERTA PRESS

GOSPEL DRUNK

Aidan Chafe

Aidan Chafe's *Gospel Drunk* is a personal journey to find clarity and identity in the face of alcoholism and religion. Sharp, intoxicating imagery and a gutsy, minimalist aesthetic combine in these poems to explore some of our darkest and strongest belief systems, dismantling them with wit and wisdom.

Robert Kroetsch Series

YOU MIGHT BE SORRY YOU READ THIS

Michelle Poirier Brown

Reveals how breaking silences and reconciling identity can refine anger into something both useful and beautiful. A poetic memoir that looks unflinchingly at childhood trauma, it also tells the story of coming to terms with a hidden Métis heritage. Honouring the complexities of Indigenous identity and the raw experiences of womanhood, mental illness, and queer selfhood, these narratives carry weight.

Robert Kroetsch Series

LITTLE WILDHEART

Micheline Maylor

"The sequence of making love and not giving a damn, the consequence of falling for and breaking off, these are Maylor's interests, and she canvasses them in indelible and fragile images, and in erudite and earthy language. Micheline Maylor is as endearing as William Carlos Williams and as dangerous as Sylvia Plath."
—George Elliott Clarke

Robert Kroetsch Series

More information at uap.ualberta.ca